The Aboli.... of Sanity

C.S. Lewis on the Consequences of Modernism

STEPHEN R. TURLEY, PH.D.

TURLEY TALKS

A New Conservative Age is Rising
www.TurleyTalks.com

Table of Contents

Introduction

In this masterful work, *The Abolition of Man,* C.S. Lewis observes how modern education is, in fact, changing our conception of what it means to be human. By sequestering the student from the objective values that formed the basis for virtue formation, modern educational practices perpetuate a mechanistic vision of the world comprised of scientifically inspired control over nature and, as a necessary consequence, humans. *The Abolition of Man* is C.S. Lewis' invitation to rediscover the doctrine of objective values and, in so doing, rediscover what it means to be truly human.

Who Was C.S. Lewis?

C live Staples Lewis, or 'Jack' as he preferred, was born on November 29, 1898, in Belfast, Northern Island, to Albert J. Lewis and Florence Augusta Hamilton. He had one older brother, Warren, who was born a couple of years prior. Shortly after his mother succumbed to cancer in 1908, Lewis was enrolled at the Wynyard School in Watford, Hertfordshire, and two years later, attended a boarding school at Campbell College, Belfast. Because of a respiratory illness, he enrolled at a prep school close to Malvern College, where he would later attend in September of 1913. He was accepted to Oxford University in 1916, but soon after, volunteered for active duty in the British Army during World War I.

He returned to Oxford and in 1925 graduated with a focus on Greek and Latin Literature and philosophy. He accepted a teaching post in English at Magdalen College, Oxford, where he remained for 29 years until he became professor of medieval and renaissance literature at Cambridge in 1954. It was during this time that Lewis rediscovered the Christian faith, largely through the influence of his colleague, J.R.R. Tolkien. And it was also during this period that he published many of his greatest works, such as *The Pilgrim's Regress* (1933), *The Great Divorce* (1945), and *The Lion, the Witch and the Wardrobe* (1950).

In 1956, he married the American writer Helen Joy Davidman, who soon became ill and died of cancer in July of 1960. Lewis died shortly thereafter on November 22, 1963 and was buried at Holy Trinity Church in Oxford. He is remembered as one of the most beloved writers and Christian apologists of all time.

The World Around

In 1928, just a few years after the end of World War I, a lecture series was founded in England that would prove to be the occasion for perhaps the most important series of lectures delivered in the 20th century. The Riddell Memorial Lectures were established in memory of Sir John Buchanan Riddell, a devout Christian, with the intention of exploring the interface between religion and contemporary thought. While a number of lectures have since been delivered, it was the Fifteenth Series of these lectures that would stamp the series indelibly on the map of intellectual history.

It was February 24th, 1943. Great Britain was in its fourth year of battle in World War II, a conflict that involved, according to then Prime Minister Winston Churchill, nothing less than the survival of Christian civilization. C.S. Lewis and his brother Warren traveled from Oxford to the small medieval town of Durham. Warren wrote in his diary that their visit to Durham was like "a little oasis in the dreariness" of their lives, an escape from the daily food rationing of urban British life in the midst of the war. This dreary, beleaguered background served an almost cliché setting for the content of Lewis' lectures over the next three evenings during the university's Epiphany term, where Lewis contrasted two antithetical futures: one in which the doctrine of objective values was embraced which assured human flourishing; the other in which such a doctrine is jettisoned in favor of scientific utilitarianism, with the consequence of humanity as we have known it abolished.

The Abolition of Man:
What Others Have Said

I ronically, in 1955, nearly a decade after it was published, Lewis wrote that *The Abolition of Man* "is almost my favourite among my books, but in general, has been almost totally ignored by the public."

Well, as it turns out, the work was not forgotten after all. Lewis' own literary executor Walter Hooper claimed that the work is "an all but indispensable introduction to the entire corpus of Lewisiana."[1] National Review chose it as number seven on their "100 Best Nonfiction Books of the Twentieth Century." The Intercollegiate Studies Institute ranked the book as the second most important work of the twentieth century. And Peter Kreeft, Professor of Philosophy at Boston College and The King's College, considers *The Abolition of Man* one of six books that if read will save Western Civilization.[2] Kreeft observes:

---

[1] Cited in Michael Travers, "The Abolition of Man: C.S. Lewis' Philosophy of History," in Bruce Edwards, ed., *C.S. Lewis: Life, Works, and Legacy, Volume 3: Apologist, Philosopher, and Theologian* (Westport, CT: Praeger, 2007), 108.
[2] http://www.intellectualtakeout.org/blog/boston-college-prof-6-books-i-would-assign-save-western-civilization.

[The Abolition of Man] is prophetic; it is couched in scholarly language; in fact, its plethora of learned Latinate references scare away even college students today, for this is the first generation in American history that is less well educated than its parents, but its content is a terrifying prophecy of mortality, not just the mortality of modern western civilization .. ... but the mortality of human nature itself if we do not recapture belief in [what Lewis calls] the *Tao*, the natural law, the doctrine of objective values.

The Abolition of Man: Summary

Published in 1944, Lewis' overall concern in *The Abolition of Man* is the state of British education in the mid-1940s. His concerns were expressed originally in three lectures over the course of three February evenings in the Physics Lecture Theatre of King's College, Newcastle, which comprise the three chapters of the book. The first chapter, entitled "Men Without Chests," draws from the classical imagery of the human person as made up of intellectual capacities, represented by the head; moral capacities, represented by the chest; and emotional and aesthetic capacities, represented by the stomach. In the classical imagination, what made us uniquely human was not the intellect since the heavenly beings had such, nor was it our appetites, which we share with the lower beasts of the earth; instead, what made us truly human was the chest, what we might call a *tertium quid,* a third thing that binds together or mediates between two otherwise unlike things. The head and the stomach, heaven and earth, come together in the chest, those moral sentiments which most characterize what it means to be human.

However, Lewis observed that modern education; that is, the education that characterized much of mid-twentieth-century

Britain, was in effect pulling apart the head from the appetites by redefining knowledge solely in terms of scientifically verified facts. Because it was supposed that facts such as '2 + 2 = 4' are value-free, in that their validity transcends any person's or culture's value system; they have no moral significance. There is no objective meaning or purpose or moral integrity in the world of facts; there are, well, only facts, nothing more.

In this modern reduction of the world as knowable only through facts, Lewis was concerned that teaching our students that the world is inherently meaningless has the effect of destroying the concept of virtue. Virtue for Lewis and the philosophers of the classical world involved ordering our loves, organizing our sentiments to reflect the divinely authored economy of goods in the world. However, Lewis was concerned that any education that denied such an economy of goods in effect denied the very basis for virtue formation. Hence, for Lewis, British education was creating a generation of young people devoid of any way of bringing their heads filled with facts together with their appetites filled with sentiment and instinct; they were creating in a word 'men without chests.'

The second chapter, entitled 'The Way,' examines three ethical theories that Lewis considers alternatives to the classical notion of a divine economy of goods. In order to demonstrate the cross-cultural significance of objective values, Lewis uses the Chinese term, the *Tao* (pronounced Dao) to denote the conception of intrinsic meaning and worth in the world. Throughout the chapter, Lewis applies the same skepticism to the three secular alternatives that modern secularists apply to the notion of objective values. As such, Lewis in effect 'relativizes the relativizer;' he calls out modern skeptics for being selective in their skepticism.

In his third chapter, 'The Abolition of Man,' Lewis sets out his vision of what a world completely governed by scientifically verified facts and devoid of any conception of the *Tao* would look like. Here, he carefully traces out the premises to their logical conclusions. For Lewis, a society rooted in technology-inspired manipulation must, by definition, organize into two classes of people: manipulators and manipulatees, or in Lewis' words, conditioners and the conditioned. Lewis recognized that technological societies succeed by convincing the masses that their highest happiness and freedom is found in their reliance on a class of experts and technicians who have the specialized competency to conform the world to their desires and ambitions. But Lewis also recognized that if all of reality has been reduced to mere nature, being understood solely through scientific facts, then even humanity itself will be seen as nothing more than mere nature. And if nature is there to be manipulated to the wants and desires of others, then inevitably the vast majority of humanity would be vulnerable to scientific and technological manipulation according to the needs of the technological elite. It is then, when man will have thought he'd finally conquered nature, that nature will have conquered man, for man as such would cease to exist; a new social order will arise that subsumes the vast majority of humanity under the category of impersonal nature which, in effect, redefines humanity as inherently meaningless; hence the title of his third chapter and the published book, the *Abolition of Man*.

The Abolition of Man:
Analysis

Men Without Chests

"I doubt whether we are sufficiently attentive to the importance of elementary textbooks."[3] (17) So Lewis begins his monumental work, *The Abolition of Man*. In the midst of its theological, philosophical, civilizational, and cultural profundities, we ought not to lose sight of the fact that *The Abolition of Man* remains centrally a book concerned with education. Lewis recognized that education ultimately is not merely informative but highly formative; education does not merely convey data and facts but shapes and molds us into a particular cultural ideal.

Lewis has this cultural ideal in mind when he begins the first chapter, "Men without Chests," by turning our attention to an episode he read in a high school English textbook, which he leaves unnamed, calling it *The Green Book*, written by two authors he also leaves unnamed, referring to them as Gaius and Titius.[4] The

---

[3] All quotes and page numbers come from C.S. Lewis, *The Abolition of Man* (New York: Simon and Schuster, 1996).

[4] We now know that the work he designated *The Green Book* was in fact the book entitled *The Control of Language*, written by Alek King and Martin

authors of this book recount the famous visit to the Waterfalls of the Clyde in Scotland taken by the poet Samuel Taylor Coleridge in the early 1800s. As Coleridge stood before the waterfall, he overheard the response of two tourists: one remarked that the waterfall was "sublime" while the other said it was "pretty." Coleridge mentally endorsed the first judgment and rejected the second with disgust.

But then Lewis relates the commentary offered by Gaius and Titius on this scene:

> When the man said that is sublime, he appeared to be making a remark about the waterfall.... Actually ... he was not making a remark about the waterfall but a remark about his own feelings. What he was saying was really I have feelings associated in my mind with the word 'Sublime,' or shortly, I have sublime feelings ... This confusion is continually present in language as we use it. We appear to be saying something very important about something: and actually, we are only saying something about our own feelings. (18)

Gaius and Titius want their readers to understand that it was actually Coleridge's aesthetic assessment that was wrong. Coleridge was mistaken in that he didn't realize that both commentaries on the waterfalls were merely expressions of subjective feelings. He, therefore, had no right, or better no basis to say that one opinion was to be preferred over another since such an evaluation would require an actual correspondence between the value that the human person places on a thing, in this case, a waterfall, and the

---

Ketley. See Jerry Root, *C.S. Lewis and a Problem of Evil: An Investigation of a Pervasive Theme* (Cambridge: James Clarke & Co., 2010), 29.

value such a thing has in and of itself, objective to or irrespective of one's opinion of it. And no such value-correspondence exists.

Education and Virtue

Lewis wastes little time in objecting to Gaius' and Titius' assessment; indeed, he appears utterly incensed that such an inane and fatuous philosophy so at odds with our human heritage could be so callously smuggled into the lives of students. Instead, Lewis appeals to a classical educational philosophy as his antidote for such brazenly irresponsible pedagogy. Lewis writes:

> The task of the modern educator is not to cut down jungles but to irrigate deserts. The right defence against false sentiments is to inculcate just sentiments. By starving the sensibility of our pupils, we only make them easier prey to the propagandist when he comes. For famished nature will be avenged, and a hard heart is no infallible protection against a soft-head. (27)

Lewis argues that it is here, in the true task of the educator, that modern education as represented by Gaius and Titius cannot but fail the student. To defend such a statement, Lewis provides an extended exploration of two fundamentally different human projects represented by two different ages or civilizations, what we might call the classical age on the one hand and the modern age on the other.

"Until quite modern times," Lewis explains, "all teachers and even all men believed the universe to be such that certain emotional reactions on our part could be either congruous or incongruous to it—believed, in fact, that objects did not merely receive, but could *merit*, our approval or disapproval, our reverence, or our contempt." (27-8)

He then summons some of history's greatest minds as witnesses to such a view of the world. In particular, he cites Augustine's conception of virtue as *ordo amoris,* the right ordering of our loves. Augustine is drawing from a similar tradition as Aristotle, who defines education as teaching the student to like and dislike what he ought. And such well-trained dispositions lead to a virtuous life. So, too, Plato in his *Republic,* who writes that the well-nurtured youth is one who loves what is truly lovely and desires what is truly desirable.

To convey the historic universality of this concept, Lewis appeals to the Chinese conception called the *Tao,* the idea that the world around us is filled with divine meaning, purpose, integrity, and, therefore, we as part of this cosmos, are all obligated to conform our lives into a harmonious relationship with that cosmic purpose. What Lewis is arguing is that this cosmic piety is true for all the major worldviews of the classical world: Platonic, Aristotelian, Stoic, Christian, and Asian. Now, these cultures may work out cosmic piety differently, with different variables and constituents that are culturally specific, but the fact that humans belong to a divine moral order appears ubiquitous throughout the ancient world.

Rejecting the *Tao*

Now, standing over against this classical vision of the world is the modern world represented by Gaius and Titius. And in this world, Lewis notes, there is only "the world of facts, without one trace of value, and the world of feelings without one trace of truth or falsehood, justice or injustice ... and no *rapprochement* is possible." (32) For Lewis, reducing all knowledge to mere scientific verification renders all value statements as mere personal preference and subjective sentiment. Because we can't put meaning under a microscope or value in a test tube, these aesthetic sentiments are sequestered from what can be known and thus rendered solely to the realm of personal opinion.

So, what becomes of education in such a world? Lewis points out that if a Roman father were to exhort his son to die for his country, he could evoke within his son a *sensibility* of the honor and nobility involved in such selfless sacrifice. Such a death is good and right because it is harmonious with the economy of goods that comprise the world in which we live. There is intrinsic worthiness to the good that calls out to us for an appropriate response.

But how would Gaius and Titius exhort their sons to die for their country? You see, Gaius and Titius can't appeal to any objective good since meaning can't be placed under a microscope. Lewis writes: "Either they must go the whole way and debunk this sentiment like any other," all honorifics associated with dying for one's country are no more than honorific feelings, "or [they] must set themselves to work to produce, from outside [the *Tao*], a sentiment which they believe to be of no value to the pupil and which may cost him his life because it is useful to us (the survivors) that our young men should feel it." (34)

Fruitful Geldings

Moreover, Lewis sees a further flaw inherent in this modern educational project. In the classical scheme of things, the human person was seen as possessing a tripartite soul made up of intellectual capacities (represented by the head), moral capacities (represented by the chest), and emotional and aesthetic capacities (represented by the stomach). What made us uniquely human was not the intellect since the heavenly beings had such, nor was it our appetites, which we shared with the lower beasts of the earth; instead, what made us truly human was the chest, what we might call a *tertium quid,* a third thing that binds together or mediates between two otherwise unlike things. The head and the stomach, heaven and earth, come together in the chest, those moral sentiments which most characterize what it means to be human. Here Lewis is drawing from a conception of the human person that goes back at least to Plato.[5] The aim of the classical educator was to bring these dimensions of the soul within students into a proper balance with one another by teaching them how to align their affections with the divine economy of goods.

However, by rejecting the *Tao,* the doctrine of objective values, the modern educator sequesters the student from the divine economy of goods by which they might order their loves. If there are no objective values to which my sentiments are to conform, then there is simply no basis for the formation of virtue such that the person loves what ought to be loved and desires what ought to be desired. And the danger here, which classical civilization recognized, is that without conforming itself to the *Tao,* to the doctrine of objective values, the human soul collapses into either unethical rationalism or unthinking sensualism. Thus, on the one hand, you have university professors like Peter Singer at Princeton who advocate infanticide (what he calls post-birth abortions) up to the age of two; on the other hand, we have today the radical pornification of pop culture.

And yet, as Lewis notes, 2,200 years of cultural and educational precedent doesn't go away overnight. It has a way of lingering in our consciences and our expectations. Thus, Lewis observes the strange irony that we in the modern age still expect these virtues to be operative in our society. We still expect honesty, courage, a commitment to the common good and human flourishing, but we

---

[5] See Plato's *Republic* 435 e8-9, 439 e3-4, and 439 d5-7.

have removed the very objective basis by which to cultivate such sentiments. Lewis writes:

> And all the time – such is the tragi-comedy of our situation – we continue to clamour for those very qualities we are rendering impossible. You can hardly open a periodical without coming across the statement that what our civilization needs is more 'drive,' or dynamism, or self-sacrifice, or 'creativity.' In a sort of ghastly simplicity, we remove the organ and demand the function. We make men without chests and expect of them virtue and enterprise. We laugh at honour and are shocked to find traitors in our midst. We castrate and bid the geldings be fruitful. (36-7)

The Way

Lewis sets out in his next chapter, "The Way," what he sees as the fundamental problem besetting any system of ethics or values that intellectuals attempt to construct irrespective of the *Tao*. If we are going to reject a world of objective moral significance, then we're going to have to come up with an alternative value system that one and the same time evokes some kind of obligation within us while acknowledging that no such obligation actually exists in the world. It's a rather tough task, and Lewis calls Gaius and Titius out on it.

Lewis begins by noting Gaius' and Titius' selective skepticism: they appear to be skeptical about all value systems save their own. Lewis will have none of it but simply applies to secular value systems the same scrutiny the skeptic applies to the *Tao*. Lewis highlights three alternatives to the *Tao*: utilitarianism, evolutionary instinct, and economic value. Though giving each one their due, he notes that there is a fundamental flaw to all three: they are all built on the assumption that we *ought* to construct our own ethical systems. But from where do we derive such a moral obligation if all moral obligations are contained *within* an alternative value construct?

For example, Lewis notes that if one says we ought to do such and such because it will preserve society, the only way such an exhortation evokes a sense of obligation is if we first *assume* that society *ought* to be preserved. Lewis notes that all ethical systems are built precisely on such assumption; they all presuppose an ethical obligation that is morally prior to the system itself. But this is precisely the *Tao,* the doctrine that all value systems are rooted in a morally defined world of which the value system is merely an *ex post facto* expression.

Here, Lewis is drawing out the significance of natural law theory, examples of which he catalogues for us in the Appendix. According to one of the foremost scholars on natural law theory, J. Budziszewski, the natural-law tradition sees the foundational principles of morality as 'the same for all, both as to rectitude and *as to knowledge'* — in other words, they are not only right for everyone but at some level, they are known to everyone."[6] Natural law theory recognizes that to be human means that we are endowed with a moral conscience which *knows* innately the moral order of the universe as God has created it.

The *Tao* defines and delineates the *oughts*, the moral obligations necessary for the intelligibility of life in a manner similar to how the laws of logic define and delineate how we ought to think. The moment we argue that we should find a system of ethics outside of the *Tao*, we are already using it; we are already assuming that we *ought* to devise an alternative set of ethics.

---

[6] http://www.acton.org/pub/religion-liberty/volume-13-number-3/natural-law-what-we-naturally-know.

The Abolition of Man

However, what happens if we do brazenly assert that the *Tao* has forever disappeared, and man can now go about the business of defining himself and his obligations in any way he so chooses? What then becomes of mankind? Lewis' final chapter, "The Abolition of Man," traces out the logical implications of a self-consciously *Tao*-less society. If we were no longer concerned about conforming our desires to the objective values embedded in the world around us but rather concerned about conforming the world to our own desires, what kind of society would emerge?

In answering this question, I think it is very important to observe that Lewis is not simply speculating here but is rather drawing premises to their logical ends. And the basic premise that Lewis expands on is a distinctively modern conception, the *summmum bonum* or man's greatest good, which involves scientifically-inspired control over nature. Our highest good, our greatest objective imaginable is the ability to conform nature to our own wants, needs, and desires. And Lewis asks, if man's control over nature were our highest good, what are the logical entailments of such an absolute commitment?

Now Lewis begins by observing right away that there seems to be a discrepancy of power over nature among a population. Lewis notes: "What we call Man's power is, in reality, a power possessed by some men which they may, or may not, allow other men to profit by.... From this point of view," Lewis writes, "what we call Man's power over Nature turns out to be a power exercised by some men over other men with Nature as its instrument." (66) Now Lewis is quick to qualify that he is not referring to mere abuses of power; he's not concerned by the ways in which power in the hands of some can be misused. Instead, he is focused on what is *logically* entailed by the orientation towards the world as an object of manipulation. If the world were there to be controlled and manipulated, does the competency for such control and manipulation necessarily extend to all men?

Lewis takes another step here: if our ultimate aim to conquer nature were to involve conquering even the *Tao,* in this case by virtue of its neglect, then mankind simply cannot be understood other than a product of nature and, therefore, a legitimate object of manipulation. Lewis sees this particularly evidenced by contraception, where earlier generations exercise control over later ones. As such, Lewis is basically arguing that in a world governed by manipulation, control, domination, there must arise by definition two classes of people: manipulators and manipulatees, or conditioners and the conditioned as he calls them. There will be those who have the technical competencies for control over nature, and then there will be the supposed beneficiaries of such competencies who, being mere products of nature, are nevertheless vulnerable to becoming objects of that control. What concerns Lewis is that if there were no longer any *Tao* by which to both separate humanity from mere nature and to foster virtue and self-control, then we are inevitably subject to the control and manipulation of others.

Now Lewis, writing in the twentieth-century follows this logic forward several centuries later; he wants us to imagine life in the hundredth century A.D., an age he speculates as the vanguard of a nihilistic society. It is one that is highly technologically sophisticated on the one hand but completely devoid of any doctrine of objective values on the other. If we trace out the discrepant pattern inherent in technological societies, this will be at a time when "the power will be exercised by a minority smaller still. Man's conquest of Nature ... means the rule of a few hundreds of men over billions upon billions of men. There neither is nor can be any simple increase of power on Man's side. Each new power won *by* man is a power *over* man as well. Each advance leaves him weaker as well as stronger." (69) In short, the more we control nature, the more we are controlled inevitably by others.

Now, the immediate objection to all of this, of course, is: Why should we suppose the men of the future to be so bad, the few ruling over the masses? Why assume the worst about them? Lewis responds that this objection simply doesn't follow the argument. Lewis writes: "I am not supposing them to be bad men. They are, rather, not men (in the old sense) at all." (73) True men operate power for good only if there is a *real good*, only if there is a real objective value to which they can and indeed must aspire. This is the world governed by *virtue,* derived from the Latin word for man, *vir.* But such a world has died under the tutelage of Gaius and Titius. That world, the world filled with divine meaning and purpose that had a right to make demands of us, that merited certain responses and demerited others, doesn't exist anymore and neither do the men of that world. They have died as well.

Lewis argues that because we have self-consciously left the world of value and virtue in favor of a world of science and technology, we have left a very definite definition of what it meant to be human for another definition of our humanity, or what Lewis might call post-humanity. Speaking of this new race, Lewis writes: "It is not that they are bad men. They are not men at all. Stepping outside the *Tao,* they have stepped into the void. Nor are their subjects necessarily unhappy men. *They* are not men at all: they are artefacts. Man's final conquest has proved to be the abolition of Man." (74)

The Irony of Idolatry

Lewis ends with the cruel irony behind all of this. In his work, *The Great Divorce,* we meet a character who actually becomes her sin; she was transforming from being a mere grumbler to be a grumble; the dehumanizing nature of idolatry is that we actually become what we worship. Lewis finishes *The Abolition of Man* with this very observation: Humanity's obsession with conquering nature has, in fact, reduced all of humanity to mere nature. Indeed, in reducing humanity to mere biological and chemical causal processes, we reduce humanity to just another natural by-product. Even the Conditioners can now only make their decisions according to nature-given desires and impulses. At that moment, then, of Man's total victory over Nature, we find the whole human race, including the Conditioners themselves, operating solely by cause-and-effect natural impulses. In attempting to conquer nature, Nature has conquered man.

Thus, Lewis concludes by calling back to the only possible solution to this inevitable abolition of our humanity:

> We have been trying, like Lear, to have it both ways: to lay down our human prerogative and yet at the same time to retain it. It is impossible. Either we are rational spirit obliged for ever to obey the absolute values of the *Tao*, or else we are mere nature to be kneaded and cut into new shapes for the pleasures of masters who must, by hypothesis, have no motive but their own 'natural' impulses. Only the *Tao* provides a common human law of action which can over-arch rulers and ruled alike. A dogmatic belief in objective value is necessary to the very idea of a rule which is not tyranny or an obedience which is not slavery. (80-81)

Lewis' solution is for us to re-embrace the *Tao*, the doctrine of objective values as the only source for our true humanity. Scientific man who believes he has evolved beyond our infantile past has been served a summons by Lewis: become once again as little children, born anew.

Famous Quotes

1. "The task of the modern educator is not to cut down jungles but to irrigate deserts. The right defence against false sentiments is to inculcate just sentiments. By starving the sensibility of our pupils we only make them easier prey to the propagandist when he comes. For famished nature will be avenged and a hard heart is no infallible protection against a soft head." (27)

2. "St Augustine defines virtue as *ordo amoris*, the ordinate condition of the affections in which every object is accorded that kind of degree of love which is appropriate to it. Aristotle says that the aim of education is to make the pupil like and dislike what he ought." (28-9)

3. "In a sort of ghastly simplicity we remove the organ and demand the function. We make men without chests and expect of them virtue and enterprise. We laugh at honour and are shocked to find traitors in our midst. We castrate and bid the geldings be fruitful." (37)

4. "A great many of those who 'debunk' traditional...values have in the background values of their own which they believe to be immune from the debunking process." (43)

5. "The *Tao*, which others may call Natural Law or Traditional Morality or the First Principles of Practical Reason or the First Platitudes, is not one among a series of possible systems of value. It is the sole source of all value judgments. If it is rejected, all value is rejected. If any value is retained, it is retained. The effort to refute it and raise a new system of value in its place is self-contradictory. There has never been, and never will be, a radically new judgment of value in the history of the world." (55)

6. "It is not that they are bad men. They are not men at all. Stepping outside the *Tao*, they have stepped into the void. Nor are their subjects necessarily unhappy men. They are not men at all: they are artefacts. Man's final conquest has proved to be the abolition of Man." (74)

7. "A dogmatic belief in objective value is necessary to the very idea of a rule which is not tyranny or an obedience which is not slavery." (81)

8. "For the wise men of old the cardinal problem had been how to conform the soul to reality, and the solution had been knowledge, self-discipline, and virtue. For magic and applied science alike the problem is how to subdue reality to the wishes of men: the solution is a technique; and both, in the practice of this technique, are ready to do things hitherto regarded as disgusting and impious — such as digging up and mutilating the dead." (83-4)

BONUS FEATURE:
Questions for Group Discussion

1. The authors of what Lewis calls *The Green Book* recount the famous visit to the Waterfalls of the Clyde in Scotland taken by the poet Samuel Taylor Coleridge in the early 1800s. For Coleridge, what was the difference between *sublime* and *pretty*?

    Pretty was a statement of one's own personal taste and preference, whereas *sublime* affirmed Beauty as an objective value embedded in a created cosmic order.

2. What's the difference between *objective* and *subjective*?

    Objective refers to that which exists outside of me and independent of my existence. *Subjective* refers to that which is specific to me. Air is objective while my lungs are subjective.

3. What were Gaius' and Titius' views on the difference between *sublime* and *pretty*?

    Gaius and Titius denied objective value in impersonal nature and located all conceptions of Beauty and sublimity to the human mind and to personal preference. Beauty is merely a subjective value constructed by the human person and superimposed on an impersonal world.

4. Can you think of biblical passages that present values as objectively part of this world?

Genesis 1 and the refrain: 'and it was good.' Note particularly Genesis 1:31: "God saw all that He had made, and behold, it was very good." The Septuagint, the early Greek translation of the Hebrew Scriptures, translated the Hebrew word *tov*, 'good,' with the Greek word *kallos*, which means 'beautiful.' The Bible speaks of certain women actually being 'beautiful' (cf. Deut 21:11; 1 Sam 25:3; 2 Sam 14:27; Prov 11:22). And Paul calls us to reflect on "whatever is true, whatever is honorable, whatever is right, whatever is pure, whatever is lovely, whatever is of good repute," and to contemplate anything "excellent and worthy of praise" (Phil 4:8).

5. Lewis writes: "The task of the modern educator is not to cut down jungles but to irrigate deserts." What does Lewis mean?

By educating the student in scientific skepticism, Gaius and Titius are reorienting the student to see the world through a hermeneutic of doubt: students are allowed to doubt and debunk anything that cannot be verified by the scientific method. However, true education seeks to awaken awe and wonder within the student by enabling him or her to see the divine meaning and purpose within the world.

6. What is Augustine's conception of *ordo amoris*?

The ordering of our loves involves matching up our sentiments in accordance with God's divine economy of goods. God has ordered the values of the world as a hierarchy that merits our affections in proportion to God's objective economy. We learn to love something in accordance with its position within that divine hierarchy. So while it is good to love a ham sandwich, it is not good to value the sandwich above the life of a baby. Virtue is in effect the right ordering of our loves so that we desire what is truly desirable.

7. Why does Lewis use the term *Tao* to denote the doctrine of objective values?

   Lewis wants to demonstrate the universality of the concept of objective values. He takes a wide range of supports as we saw – Platonic, Aristotelian, Jewish, Christian, Confucian, etc – and then formulates basically a bumper sticker definition of a term that encapsulates this wide range of support.

8. How does the modern world define *knowledge* differently from the classical world?

   Knowledge in the classical world included theological and moral understandings of the *Tao,* the doctrine of objective values. Knowledge in the modern world has been reduced largely to scientific rationalism, which can only see the world in terms of biological, chemical, and physical causal processes.

9. In light of classical education's commitment to the *Tao,* why is Lewis so concerned about modern education?

   In teaching students that the world is made up solely of biological, chemical, and physical causal processes, modern education has removed any objective value system whereby we might order our loves. Modern education is thus devoid of any basis for virtue formation.

10. What does Lewis mean by modern education creating 'men without chests'?

   In the classical imagination, what made us uniquely human was not the intellect since the heavenly beings had such, nor was it our appetites, which we share with the lower beasts of the earth; instead, what made us truly human was the chest, what we might call a *tertium quid,* a third thing that binds together or mediates between two otherwise unlike things. The head and the stomach, heaven and earth, come together in the chest, those moral sentiments which most characterize what it means to be human. Without a basis for virtue formation, modern education is devoid of that which can bring head and stomach together.

11. Lewis begins chapter two, 'The Way,' by writing: "However subjective they may be about some traditional value, Gaius and Titius have shown by the very act of writing *The Green Book* that there must be some other values about which they are not subjective at all." What does he mean by this?

The only way one can sweep away any value system is with an alternative value system.

12. How does Lewis 'relativize the relativizer' in the second chapter?

He applies the same skepticism towards the skeptic's proposed value system that the skeptic applies to the doctrine of objective values. Were the skeptic's critique of objective values actually valid, it would undermine equally any alternative value system he himself put forward.

13. What is utilitarianism, and is Lewis' critique of it?

Utilitarianism is the notion that something is valuable only if it is useful to one or many. If something is of no use, it has no valid moral compulsion. Lewis notes that there's nothing inherently obligatory in utilitarianism. The utilitarian has to assume that we ought to define our values in accordance with utilitarian norms.

14. What is natural law theory, and how does Lewis employ it in his argument?

Natural law theory recognizes that to be human means that we are endowed with a moral conscience which *knows* innately the moral order of the universe as God has created it. The moral obligations that serve as imperatives to our human conduct are rationally discernible irrespective of one's religious tradition. Lewis notes that every proposed value system is built on an assumption that we *ought* to have value systems. Thus our value systems are always derivative of some kind of moral obligation that exists outside of those systems.

15. What is Lewis' critique of evolutionary instinct?

We have to first assume that our instinctive dispositions are in fact good. But how are we obligated to obey instinct? Are all instincts equally valid? If not, then how can mutually exclusive instincts be adjudicated by just another instinct? Moreover, if instincts were the inevitable arbiters of ethical choices, why then are *Green Books* written in the first place?

16. Throughout this chapter, Lewis argues that we can't extrapolate an *ought* from an *is*. What does he mean by that?

Just because a state of affairs exists doesn't mean such a state *ought* to exist. 'Is' does not entail 'ought,' they are conceptually quite different. This is what's known as a *non sequitur,* or something that does not follow from the premise.

17. How does Lewis describe the difference between the classical conception of the world and the modern conception?

Lewis summarizes the difference between a classical conception of the world and the modern conception this way: For classical man, the fundamental question was: How do I conform my soul to the world around me and thus be drawn up into divine life? and the answer was through prayer, virtue, and knowledge. However, for modern man, the question is inverted: modern man is not interested in how to conform the soul to reality; rather modern man asks: How do I conform the world to my own desires and ambitions? and the answer involves tapping into those institutions that operate by the mechanisms of power and manipulation, namely, science, technology, and the state.

18. Lewis argues that a society founded on science and technology must by definition evolve into two classes of people. What are those two classes and why are they necessary?

The two classes of people are what Lewis calls *conditioners* and the *conditioned.* Lewis believes that as more and more people become dependent on technological expertise, technocracies are inevitably ruled by technical experts who convince the masses that such competencies are the basis for the freedom and prosperity.

19. What is the danger of such a society?

If there were no longer any *Tao* by which to both separate humanity from mere nature and to foster virtue and *self-control*, then we are inevitably subject to the control and manipulation of others. We are by definition no different from nature, and as nature is there to be controlled and manipu-lated, then humans are legitimate objects of control and manipulation.

20. Regarding the conditioners, Lewis writes: "I am not supposing them to be bad men. They are, rather, not men (in the old sense) at all." What does he mean?

The classical conception of man involved the cultivation of virtue, derived from the Latin word for man, *vir*. But such a world has died under the tutelage of Gaius and Titius. That world, the world filled with divine meaning and purpose that had a right to make demands of us, that merited certain responses and demerited others, doesn't exist anymore, and neither do the men of that world. They have died as well.

21. Lewis reflects on the relationship between four practices: science, technology, religion, and magic. How and why did the medieval world pair these practices so differently from the modern world?

The medieval world defined knowledge as comprised of natural revelation and special revelation, or science and religion. Both science and religion sought to understand the world, while magic and technology sought to manipulate the world in some way. The modern age, devoted as it is to using knowledge as a means by which to manipulate nature, has married science with technology as the two primary ways in which its new *summum bonum* might be realized. Magic and religion are impervious to the modern quest for control.

Further Considerations

"I doubt whether we are sufficiently attentive to the importance of elementary text books." This is how Lewis begins his monumental work, *The Abolition of Man*. Reflect on Lewis' statement in light of classical education project known as *paideia,* which sought to initiate students into a culture. Is it possible to have education without some kind of *paideia*?

Why did Lewis begin his entire discussion with the scene from the Waterfalls of the Clyde? How is such a scene a microcosm of the entire book?

What is 'education'? Can a secular worldview provide a true education?

What is your assessment of natural law? Is it biblical? If so, how?

How would you explain the rational coherence of moral obligation to someone apart from an appeal to the Bible?

Reflect on the relationship between public education's commitment to teaching students that truth is relative on the one hand and the assumed dishonesty of politicians on the other. How is this an example of Lewis' concern that 'we have removed the organ but still demand the function'? Can you think of other examples?

Think of other socially constructed alternatives to the *Tao* than the three provided by Lewis. Do they fall victim to the same critiques offered in second chapter? Why?

Lewis contends that we can't derive an *ought* from an *is*. Do you agree? Why or why not?

Do you share Lewis' bleak outlook on what a *Tao*-less future would look like? How does Lewis' vision compare to Aldous Huxley's *Brave New World* or George Orwell's *1984*?

Thank you again for purchasing this book!

I hope this book not only enlightened you by showing you the consequences of modernism but encouraged you by lighting the pathway back to civilizational flourishing.

If you enjoyed this book, then I'd like to ask you for a favor: Would you be kind enough to leave a review for this book on Amazon? I would so greatly appreciate it!

Thank you so much, and may God richly bless you!

Steve Turley

www.turleytalks.com

Check Out My Other Books

Below you'll find some of my other popular books that are popular on Amazon. Simply go to the links below to check them out. Alternatively, you can visit my author page on Amazon to see my other works.

- *The Return of Christendom: Demography, Politics, and the Coming Christian Majority* https://amzn.to/2VM2W4O

- *The New Nationalism: How the Populist Right is Defeating Globalism and Awakening a New Political Order* https://amzn.to/2WEP11u

- *The Triumph of Tradition: How the Resurgence of Religion is Reawakening a Conservative World* https://amzn.to/2xieNO3

- *Classical vs. Modern Education: A Vision from C.S. Lewis* http://amzn.to/2opDZju

- *President Trump and Our Post-Secular Future: How the 2016 Election Signals the Dawning of a Conservative Nationalist Age* http://amzn.to/2B87Q22

- *Gazing: Encountering the Mystery of Art* https://amzn.to/2yKi6k9

- *Beauty Matters: Creating a High Aesthetic in School Culture* https://amzn.to/2L8Ejd7

- *Ever After: How to Overcome Cynical Students with the Role of Wonder in Education* http://amzn.to/2jbJI78

- *Movies and the Moral Imagination: Finding Paradise in Films* http://amzn.to/2zjghJj

- *Echoes of Eternity: A Classical Guide to Music*
  https://amzn.to/2O0bYrY

- *Health Care Sharing Ministries: How Christians are Revolutionizing Medical Cost and Care* http://amzn.to/2B2Q8B2

- *The Face of Infinite of Love: Athanasius on the Incarnation* http://amzn.to/2oxULNM

- *Stressed Out: Learn How an Ancient Christian Practice Can Relieve Stress and Overcome Anxiety* http://amzn.to/2kFzcpc

- *Wise Choice: Six Steps to Godly Decision Making* http://amzn.to/2qy3C2Z

- *Awakening Wonder: A Classical Guide to Truth, Goodness, and Beauty* http://amzn.to/2ziKR5H

- *Worldview Guide for* A Christmas Carol http://amzn.to/2BCcKHO

- *The Ritualized Revelation of the Messianic Age: Washings and Meals in Galatians and 1 Corinthians* http://amzn.to/2B0mGvf

If the links do not work, for whatever reason, you can simply search for these titles on the Amazon website to find them.

About www.TurleyTalks.com

Are we seeing the revitalization of Christian civilization?

For decades, the world has been dominated by a process known as globalization, an economic and political system that hollows out and erodes a culture's traditions, customs, and religions, all the while conditioning populations to rely on the expertise of a tiny class of technocrats for every aspect of their social and economic lives.

Until now.

All over the world, there's been a massive blowback against the anti-cultural processes of globalization and its secular aristocracy. From Russia to Europe and now in the U.S., citizens are rising up and reasserting their religion, culture, and nation as mechanisms of resistance against the dehumanizing tendencies of secularism and globalism.

And it's just the beginning.

The secular world is at its brink, and a new traditionalist age is rising.

Join me each week as we examine these worldwide trends, discover answers to today's toughest challenges, and together learn to live in the present in light of even better things to come.

So hop on over to www.TurleyTalks.com and have a look around. Make sure to sign-up for our weekly Email Newsletter where you'll get lots of free giveaways, private Q&As, and tons of great content. Check out our YouTube channel (www.youtube.com/c/DrSteveTurley) where you'll understand current events in light of conservative trends to help you flourish in your personal and professional life. And of course, 'Like' us on Facebook and follow us on Twitter.

Thank you so much for your support and for your part in this cultural renewal.

About the Author

S teve Turley (PhD, Durham University) is an internationally recognized scholar, speaker, and classical guitarist. He is the author of over a dozen books, including *Classical vs. Modern Education: A Vision from C.S. Lewis, Awakening Wonder: A Classical Guide to Truth, Goodness, and Beauty,* and *The Ritualized Revelation of the Messianic Age: Washings and Meals in Galatians and 1 Corinthians.* Steve's popular YouTube channel showcases weekly his expertise in the rise of nationalism, populism, and traditionalism throughout the world, and his podcasts and writings on civilization, society, culture, education, and the arts are widely accessed at TurleyTalks.com. He is a faculty member at Tall Oaks Classical School in Bear, DE, where he teaches Theology and Rhetoric, and was formerly Professor of Fine Arts at Eastern University. Steve lectures at universities, conferences, and churches throughout the U.S. and abroad. His research and writings have appeared in such journals as *Christianity and Literature, Calvin Theological Journal, First Things, Touchstone,* and *The Chesterton Review.* He and his wife, Akiko, have four children and live in Newark, DE, where they together enjoy fishing, gardening, and watching *Duck Dynasty* marathons.

Printed in Great Britain
by Amazon